SNOW LEOPARDS

BIG CATS

BY DIANNA DORISI-WINGET

Consultant: Christina Simmons
San Diego Zoo Global
San Diego, California

CAPSTONE PRESS
a capstone imprint

Edge Books are published by Capstone Press,
1710 Roe Crest Drive, North Mankato, Minnesota 56003.
www.capstonepub.com

Library of Congress Cataloging-in-Publication Data
Dorisi-Winget, Dianna.
  Snow leopards / by Dianna Dorisi-Winget.
    p. cm. — (Edge books. Big cats)
  Includes bibliographical references and index.
  ISBN 978-1-4296-7645-8 (library binding)
1. Snow leopard—Juvenile literature. I. Title.
  QL737.C23D66 2012
  599.75'55—dc23   2011021018

Summary: "Describes the history, physical features, and habitat of snow leopards"
—Provided by publisher.

Editorial Credits
Brenda Haugen, editor; Kyle Grenz, designer; Svetlana Zhurkin,
    media researcher; Laura Manthe, production specialist

Photo Credits
Alamy: Rick Dalton Wildlife, 7, Skip Higgins of Raskal Photography, 22, Terry
Whittaker, 17, 20–21; Creatas, 10 (top); Dreamstime: Seread, 11, Shargaljut, 27
(left); National Geographic Stock: Minden Pictures/Cyril Ruoso, 18, Steve Winter,
4, 8; Nature Picture Library/Eric Dragesco, 9; Photo courtesy of Snow Leopard
Trust, 5, 26 (right), 27 (right), Rod Jackson, 24; Shutterstock: BMCL, 10 (bottom),
chiakto, 26 (left), Dmitri Gomon, 13, Glen Gaffney, 28, J van der Wolf, 12, James
Steidl, 29, Karen Kane, Alberta, Canada, 14–15, ludo, 16, Mark Bridger, 19, Peter
Wey, 25, S.R. Maglione, 1, Scott E. Read, 6, Stanislav Eduardovich Petrov
(background), throughout, Steve Wilson, cover, Svetlana Yudina, 23, Tony Rix, 15

Printed in the United States of America in North Mankato, Minnesota.
012013   007146R

TABLE OF CONTENTS

Chapter 1

GHOST OF THE MOUNTAIN

Two scientists stood on a bitterly cold mountain slope in Mongolia, a country in Asia. They scanned the opposite mountain ridge with binoculars. The steady beeping of a snow leopard's radio collar told them the big cat was very near. Why couldn't they spot this big **predator**? All they could see was swirling snow and foggy cliffs.

Big Cat Fact

Snow leopards make a lot of sounds. They may hiss, meow, growl, and make other noises. However, they can't roar.

4

After scanning the slope a long time, the frustrated scientists gave up. The beeping from the cat's collar had grown silent. Once again the big cat, known as "the ghost of the mountain," had somehow escaped without being seen.

Hiding from People

People have a big effect on how snow leopards live. In general, snow leopards are most active around sunrise and sunset. In areas where there are few people, snow leopards may be active during the day too. In places where there are many people, snow leopards may be most active at night. The big cats try to avoid any contact with people.

predator—an animal that hunts other animals for food

BIG BUT ALMOST INVISIBLE

Snow leopards are big cats. An adult snow leopard weighs between 60 and 120 pounds (27 and 54 kilograms). It stands about 2 feet (0.6 meter) tall at the shoulder. It stretches 6 to 7.5 feet (1.8 to 2.3 m) from its head to the base of its tail.

Big Cat Fact

Snow leopards have the longest tails of any cats. A snow leopard's tail is about as long as its body.

Size Comparison Chart

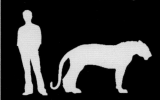

The average height of an American male is 5 feet, 10 inches (178 centimeters).

A snow leopard's markings make it almost invisible in its snowy mountain **habitat**. Most of its body is covered with gray-yellow fur. Its stomach, chest, and chin are creamy white. This coloring allows a snow leopard to blend in against the misty clouds and snow. A snow leopard's big, dark spots help it disappear among shady rock cliffs. Even animal herders who share the snow leopards' mountain home rarely see the big cats.

habitat—the natural place and conditions in which an animal or plant lives

Big Cat Fact

Snow leopards often spend several days in the same area, but they can cover hundreds of miles in a week.

LEAVING CLUES

Signs of snow leopards are almost as hard to find as the big cats themselves. To figure out how many of the big cats live in a certain area, scientists look for tracks and **scat**. Scientists also look for urine marks sprayed on rocks. A snow leopard may spray urine on rocks near nose level so other snow leopards can easily smell their markings. The smell lets other snow leopards know the territory is taken.

scat—animal droppings

a snow leopard scrape

Big Cat Fact

Scientists also search for scrapes the animals make to mark their territories. To make a scrape, a snow leopard digs at the ground with its back legs. It creates small dips and a mound.

Snow leopards live in snowy mountainous regions in Central Asia. Scientists believe that only 3,500 to 7,000 snow leopards are living in the wild. Another 600 to 700 live in zoos.

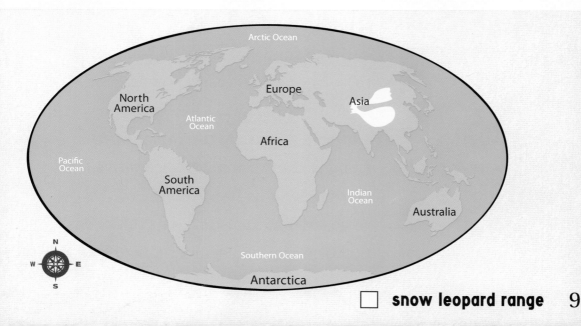

☐ **snow leopard range**

KEEPING WARM

Snow leopards spend most of their lives high in the mountains at heights of between 9,000 and 19,700 feet (2,743 and 6,005 m). At these heights, snow leopards face short summers and long, harsh winters. During late autumn, snow begins to fall, and a snow leopard's fur coat grows up to 5 inches (12.7 centimeters) long. A snow leopard's long, thick fur helps it survive cold temperatures.

Deep snow poses no problem for these big cats either. A snow leopard's large, broad paws act like snowshoes and help it walk on top of snowdrifts. Long fur between a snow leopard's toes helps protect its feet from the cold snow. A snow leopard also uses its thick, bushy tail for warmth. The big cat wraps its tail around its face and body like a scarf.

Snow leopards are well adapted to the cold. But winter is still a tough time. Food is scarce. During this season, snow leopards are most likely to attack livestock.

Chapter 2

ON THE HUNT

What a snow leopard eats depends on the types of animals that live in the big cat's territory.

One of a snow leopard's most common **prey** is ibex, a type of wild goat. Snow leopards also eat blue sheep found in the Himalayan Mountains and Tibet. They also eat musk deer and smaller animals such as marmots, hares, and birds.

ibex

prey—an animal hunted by another animal for food

Although snow leopards mainly eat meat, they sometimes eat plants. Scientists have found that snow leopards eat grass, twigs, and other plant material. Snow leopards eat plants most often during mating season. Scientists believe that plants could provide snow leopards with extra vitamins. Plants may also aid with digestion or help snow leopards get rid of **parasites**.

parasite—an animal or plant that lives on or inside another plant or animal

ESCAPE ME IF YOU CAN

A snow leopard's hunting ability shows how well adapted the big cat is to its habitat. Big lungs give snow leopards enough oxygen to live at high altitudes. Long, muscular hind legs allow these cats to leap up to 30 feet (9 m). A long tail helps a snow leopard keep its balance as it makes fast, sharp turns while chasing prey.

Big Cat Fact

A snow leopard can kill prey that is three times its size.

A snow leopard prefers to pounce onto prey from higher ground. The big cat grips its prey with razor-sharp claws. Then it kills the animal with a bite to the prey's throat or the back of its neck. A snow leopard's long, powerful teeth are designed to grab, rip, and shred meat. A snow leopard's teeth can chomp right through bones and hide.

Prey Problems

If wild prey is hard to find, snow leopards may kill ranchers' livestock. Snow leopards have entered corrals and killed sheep, goats, horses, and yaks. This has caused problems for ranchers in places such as Mongolia.

DINNERTIME

Snow leopards eat slowly. They may take three or four days to eat large prey, such as sheep or ibex. During that time the snow leopard stays near the kill. The big cat protects it from vultures or other animals that might try to steal it. But snow leopards are not **aggressive** toward people. Even if disturbed while eating, a snow leopard is far more likely to run from a person than to stay and defend its kill. It is more likely for a snow leopard to become aggressive if it feels threatened or thinks its cubs are in danger.

A Big Appetite

marmot

Snow leopards need a lot of prey to survive. They seem to prefer a variety of prey. A snow leopard living in a national park in India proved that. It ate five blue sheep, nine Tibetan woolly hares, 25 marmots, five goats, one domestic sheep, and more than a dozen birds in one year.

Big Cat Fact

There's no record of a snow leopard attacking a person.

Chapter 3

RAISING YOUNG

Male and female snow leopards develop at different rates. Female snow leopards may have their first **litter** of cubs when they are 2 or 3 years old. Males can begin mating when they are 4 years old.

Males and females mate between January and the middle of March. Mating season is the only time adult female and male snow leopards are found together.

HAVING CUBS

Because snow leopards are so shy and **elusive**, not much is known about the behavior of pregnant females. In captivity female snow leopards seek out hidden places to give birth. Once a female finds a spot she likes, she lines it with her fur. Researchers believe that wild snow leopards behave the same way.

Females give birth after about 95 to 100 days. Cubs are born in the spring or early summer. A mother usually gives birth to two or three cubs.

elusive—clever at hiding

GROWING UP

Cubs are born helpless. Their eyes are closed until they are about 1 week old. By about 6 weeks of age, cubs eat solid food. When they are strong enough, the young leopards begin following their mother around. They explore and learn important skills to help them survive in the wild. When the cubs are 3 months old, their mother starts teaching them to hunt.

A female snow leopard mates only every two years. She spends between 18 and 22 months raising one litter of cubs.

LIFE SPAN

Snow leopards in zoos have lived more than 20 years. No one knows for sure how long wild snow leopards live. But researchers believe wild snow leopards have shorter life spans than those in **captivity** because wild snow leopards have harder lives.

captivity—the condition of being kept in a cage

Chapter 4

ON THE BRINK

Snow leopards are **endangered** animals.
Poaching presents a big threat to their survival.
Poachers earn a great deal of money by selling
snow leopard bones and fur. Snow leopard
bones are used to make medicine in China.
Snow leopard fur is used to make a variety
of items, including coats.

endangered—at risk of dying out

poach—to hunt or fish ilegally

People threaten the survival of snow leopards in other ways too. People hunt the same prey snow leopards do, including ibex and blue sheep. Farmers sometimes poison marmots and other prey because farmers view them as pests. The less wild prey the snow leopard has, the more likely it is to kill livestock. Then local ranchers respond by killing the snow leopards.

People also cause problems by shrinking the cats' habitat. As more people move into snow leopard territory, less habitat is available to the big cats. A shrinking habitat forces snow leopards into closer contact with people and livestock.

PROTECTION EFFORTS

The way people feel about snow leopards has improved over time. In many countries people are starting to value the big cats and offer them protection.

Snow Leopard Enterprises formed in 1998. This group encourages Mongolian ranching families to make products such as wool socks, mittens, scarves, and yarn. These products are sold in the United States and other countries at stores, special events, and online.

The money made from the sale of the products goes to the families who make the items. But only families who promise not to kill snow leopards or the prey of leopards can join the program. Most of the families use the money they earn to buy rice, flour, or other food. Some families have made enough money to send their children to school or to buy medicine. More than 350 families participate in the program.

WHY PROTECTION MATTERS

Studies of snow leopards have shown that they need our respect and protection. There are many reasons to protect these rare cats. Removing a predator such as the snow leopard can upset nature's balance. Without predators, prey animals can become too plentiful and spread disease. These diseases can sometimes make livestock sick.

Big Penalties

The Convention on International Trade in Endangered Species makes it illegal to take snow leopard parts across any country's border. Anyone trying to take a snow leopard skin into the United States faces a $25,000 fine. Other countries' laws are even stricter. For example, bringing a snow leopard skin to Nepal could lead to five to 15 years in jail.

Even the numbers and kinds of **microorganisms** in the soil can be changed if the balance between predators and prey is upset. Changes in the soil could harm crops or damage habitat. The world would never be the same if these ghosts of the mountains disappeared forever.

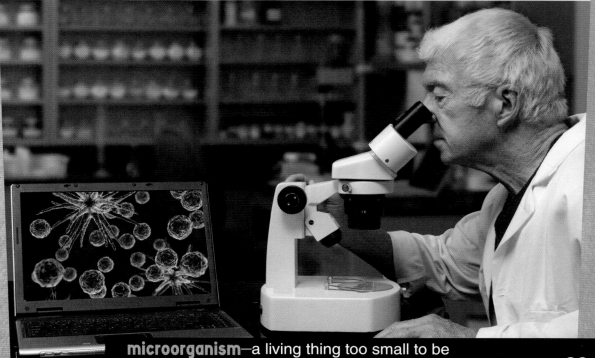

microorganism—a living thing too small to be seen without a microscope

GLOSSARY

aggressive (uh-GREH-siv)—strong and forceful

captivity (kap-TIV-ih-tee)—the condition of being kept in a cage

elusive (ee-LOO-siv)—clever at hiding

endangered (in-DAYN-juhrd)—at risk of dying out

habitat (HAB-uh-tat)—the natural place and conditions in which an animal or plant lives

litter (LIT-ur)—a group of animals born at the same time to one mother

microorganism (mye-kro-OR-gan-iz-um)—a living thing too small to be seen without a microscope

parasite (PAIR-uh-site)—an animal or plant that lives on or inside another animal or plant

poach (POHCH)—to hunt or fish illegally

predator (PRED-uh-tur)—an animal that hunts other animals for food

prey (PRAY)—an animal hunted by another animal for food

scat (SKAT)—animal droppings

READ MORE

Magellan, Marta. *Those Colossal Cats.* Those Amazing Animals. Sarasota, Fla.: Pineapple Press, 2009.

Montgomery, Sy. *Saving the Ghost of the Mountain: An Expedition among Snow Leopards in Mongolia.* Scientists in the Field. Boston: Houghton Mifflin Books for Children, 2009.

Turner, Pamela S. *A Life in the Wild: George Schaller's Struggle to Save the Last Great Beasts.* New York: Farrar, Straus, and Giroux, 2008.

INTERNET SITES

FactHound offers a safe, fun way to find Internet sites related to this book. All of the sites on FactHound have been researched by our staff.

Here's all you do:

Visit *www.facthound.com*

Type in this code: 9781429676458

Super-cool stuff! Check out projects, games and lots more at
www.capstonekids.com

INDEX